To DENNIS.

FOND MEMO?

CW00538946

Another Sound of Music

The Poole Family

Cyril Poole

Cyril Poole

Sylvia.

Yorkshire Art Circus
in association with
Wakefield MDC
(Housing Services)

1993

Published by Yorkshire Art Circus
in association with
Smawthorne & Glasshoughton Renewal
Wakefield MDC (Housing Services)

Yorkshire Art Circus
School Lane, Glasshoughton, Castleford.
West Yorkshire WF10 4QH
Telephone (0977) 550401

Edited by Fiona Edwards, Brian Lewis and Joan Thornton

Cover design: Tadpole Graphics

ISBN : 0 947780 91 2
Classification: Autobiography

Technical support: Pam Davenport, Olive Fowler and Reini Schühle

Photographs: Chris Hodgson
                Pontefract & Castleford Express
                Yorkshire Television

Printed by: Emka Print, 10 Baileygate, Industrial Estate, Pontefract

We would like to thank the following organisations for support
towards this book:

Wakefield MDC (Housing Services),
Wakefield MDC (Leisure),
West Yorkshire Grants and
Yorkshire & Humberside Arts

Cyril Poole

Sylvia and Cyril, married 23 January, 1954

Chapter One

October 1976, and the estate agent had let me in. I was looking for the last time at 96 Ferrybridge Road, the house that had thrived on the sound of music. This is where the family had rehearsed round the piano, entertained visitors from record companies, television and the press when the Poole Family of Castleford was a household name.

Arcadia is on one of the main roads out of Castleford, away from the swirling fumes of chemical factories, up the big hill and past Queen's Park, the town's pride and joy, up right to the very top of Red Hill. From there it looks down on the town from a plateau, standing above all Castleford's rehousing and development of the fifties. Down below is the old town of back-to-back houses, chimneys, factories and workshops.

Our house was right opposite the main park gates. You could look out of our front room window on to the lovely colours of the flower beds. The drive was shared by four houses, two pairs of semis. The Borough Treasurer was my immediate neighbour and to the left of the drive was the Deputy Town Clerk and his neighbour, Police Sergeant King. We lived in trepidation of these people when we first got there, but as it turned out they were very ordinary, like us.

Arcadia was our home between 1972 and 1976. With four girls and three boys, Sylvia and I had, during these years, made sure that this house thrived on the sound of music. I can't ever remember coming in or going out without the sound of the hi-fi or even live music somewhere in the house.

Half way up our garden was a large beech tree about forty feet high. In its branches I made a platform and was just as thrilled as the children at being able to climb on to it. In secret we would overlook the people walking up and down Ferrybridge Road and on a quiet Sunday morning blow an old Boys' Brigade bugle. Unsuspecting neighbours would try in vain to find where this unusual sound was coming from.

The house in which the kids spent their formative years, the one in which they organised a ghost attic and where they taught each other the lyrics they needed as principal acts in Junior Showtime and Stars on

Sunday - today I was looking at it for the last time.

*

We weren't born to big houses or to making money from popular music though in the glorious fifties when I was only seventeen, nothing but a lad serving my apprenticeship as a painter and decorator, I loved dance band music. I envied the singers who stepped forward, adjusted the height of the mike to give a rendition of Dickie Valentine's Mr Sandman or Lita Rosa's Sugar Bush.

When I was at work spreading paint on some uninteresting office wall, my paint brush would beat out the rhythm and my voice could be heard all over the building. Empty offices provided a perfect echo chamber. I knew all the latest songs and thought I was good. I entered talent shows with a lot of success and my confidence grew.

I learned to dance and on Saturday nights we would go to Normanton Baths where the Council would cover the swimming pool with a sprung wooden floor. A stage appeared at the far end where the diving table normally towered, and Ernie Richardson and his Dance Band would play.

We paid at the same window where we got our tickets, for swimming; half a crown in old money, the equivalent to twelve and a half new pence today. As we walked through the double doors into the dance area we met the warmth, the smell of perfume and the coloured lights. The girls wore taffeta ballerina length dance dresses or skirts in pastel colours with an overdress of black lace. These were covered in sequins and picked up the light from the revolving mirror ball that hung from the ceiling in the centre of the dance floor. The lads all wore smart suits, some were pinstripes, others were plain, and all had clean white shirts. Hairstyles varied from centre parting to large quiffs and some even wore the new 'DA' style - swept up at the sides and meeting at the back in a neat parting. 'DA' referred to the rear end of a duck.

Hardly anyone had cars so travelling to dance halls was limited to local areas and everyone knew one another. Most people could do the basic steps of ballroom dancing and there was always somebody ready to teach newcomers. When you first went dancing the lads would stand round in groups watching the girls who danced round together. After a time you would say to your mate, "Let's split these two," and you would walk up and ask, "Mind if I dance with you?" Then you would take one and dance with her to the end, chatting away, asking her name and introducing yourself. Most of it was small talk but if you liked the girl you would ask, "Is it alright if I get you up again?"

No girl ever approached a boy but you could see girls dancing round together and looking round the room for lads to split them. The signals were obvious if you were welcome.

Some of us used to go to the youth club on Thursday nights for Bill Higson's dancing lessons and on Saturday nights we put our new steps into practice. I liked girls but the real magic for me was the music. I loved to hold a girl in my arms and dance round the floor, crooning the hits of the moment.

That's where I met Sylvia. She was a good dancer. I knew that from seeing her and her friend June, so whenever I got the chance I would dance with her. Unlike a lot of girls, she always had plenty to talk about while we danced.

I would say things like, "Are you still going out with Harry?" She would reply, "Oh yes, but you know he's in the army and he hasn't any leave this weekend. Are you still going out with Irene?"

"No. I found out she was courting a sailor so I dropped her pretty sharp. I'm knocking about with Megan. You know, that nurse that goes to the youth club. She's working this weekend."

After that sort of chat I would swirl her round and sing a Bing Crosby song in her ear.

Most of our group of friends belonged to the youth club and dancing class, so it wasn't unusual at the weekend to go as a group to the dance, especially as some of the lads were in the Forces. In those years girls were never short of partners. It never crossed my mind to ask Sylvia out for a date even though I liked her a lot. She had a jolly personality, she liked to laugh and we got on very well as dancing partners. She was a girl I respected and I enjoyed her company. We were old friends from our school days, Sylvia came from Old Snydale, a small village just out of Normanton. Her grandfather was the landlord at The Cross Keys, a pub to which my mother and father used to walk on summer afternoons, pushing me in the pram. There they would stop for a drink and one of Sylvia's mum's home-made ice creams. Our first meeting was in prams parked together.

Sylvia was a good looking girl, enough to turn any man's head for a second look, but I danced with other girls and she danced with other boys, and the relationship was no more than that.

I used to go dancing, keeping the flag flying on the dance floor for Derek

7

Bowles and Charlie Hollie, pals who were called up for National Service. I was serving an apprenticeship so I had my calling up deferred until I was twenty-one. One Saturday Derek, who'd gone into the RAF, called round. He was home on leave unexpectedly and this changed the plans of June, his girlfriend. Because Sylvia lived in a rural village with no lights and very little public transport, it meant her sleeping the night at June's house.

"Will you make up a foursome and take Sylvia to the dance?" Derek asked. I jumped at the chance. It was during the course of that evening that I found out that Sylvia hadn't got a steady boyfriend.

As I was dancing with her I plucked up the courage and asked, "Will I be able to take you out tomorrow?"

Her answer took me by surprise. "You're joking," she said. I didn't know what she meant and thought I had blown it, but she was just as taken aback by the question. She soon corrected herself and said, "Yes."

I was over the moon. I couldn't understand why I had never thought of asking her before, perhaps I hadn't wanted to spoil a good friendship. After that our relationship grew. Instead of just going out to the dance together we met at every opportunity. Most lunchtimes I would ring Sylvia at the Pontefract office where she worked. I'd got it bad.

We were both attending night school in Wakefield; I was taking practical painting and decorating, signwriting and heraldry; and Sylvia, who worked in a drawing office for the Town and Country Planning, was taking a course on map tracing. Since she also went for other courses like leatherwork and cake decorating at the same college, we were able to meet after classes too. Soon we met each other's families and were each made very welcome by both sides.

We often went out in a foursome with Derek and June and sometimes my brother Les and his wife Mary joined us too. In the summer of 1952 the six of us went on holiday to Blackpool and saw the big dance bands at the Tower Ballroom and the Winter Gardens. Ted Heath, Joe Loss and Geraldo played, each with their own vocalists, as we danced the night away. We never missed Reginald Dixon playing at the Tower Ballroom on his famous Wurlitzer Organ that appeared through the stage floor as he played Oh, I Do Like to Be Beside the Seaside. It was all exciting but there is a permanent picture which will live forever in my mind - on the balconies were the names of all the great and famous composers and above the magnificent stage the inscription in gold lettering Bid Me Discourse And I Will Enchant Thine Ear. It made the hairs on my arms bristle.

Yet for all the romance of the strange surroundings there were still echoes of home.

During our week's holiday we were strolling along the Central Pier when we were attracted to a large crowd assembling in the open air theatre. We pushed our way to the front and, to our amazement, found the star attraction was a pal of ours from the dance hall back home. Wearing tight trousers, a long coat and blue suede shoes with three inch crepe soles, his legs gyrating all over the place, Vic Rushton from Normanton was demonstrating with his girlfriend the new Be-Bop dance.

Blackpool was a very special place for me and Sylvia. The following year we spent another week there going dancing every night. During one romantic evening while we were dancing to the Ted Heath Band and Dickie Valentine was singing Too Young, I said to Sylvia, "I think it's time we got married, don't you?"

She went quiet for a moment and then said, "Well, yes, but I don't know if our parents will agree."

When we got home I somehow didn't get round to asking, but later that year nature decided we should get married so I had the awesome task of asking the parents under duress. Sylvia was a bit upset because this wasn't the way she had wanted to start her married life, but to my surprise and delight, both sets of parents were very understanding. The wedding took place on Saturday, 23rd January 1954 at North Featherstone Parish Church.

The words of the song on the night that I had proposed to Sylvia were a pointer to our future -

They try to tell us we're too young,
Too young to really be in love,
And then someday they may recall,
We were not too young at all.

*

Sylvia was nineteen and I was twenty when we got married, but we were in love with stars in our eyes.

Like many young people who married in those days we lived with parents. It was a small prefab and we had the front bedroom which I decorated in pink and blue. Sylvia and I both paid two pounds for board to my mother and it was a good arrangement because Sylvia and my mum got on very well together.

Stephen was born on June 10th, 1954 at the Maternity Home in Barnes

Road, Castleford. He was five weeks premature and Sylvia had to stay in the maternity home until he was over five pounds in weight. For nearly a month I went to visit her nightly and took her out for a walk after she had fed the baby. It was just like courting again. When she came home and brought the baby, both Mum and Dad worshipped him. Those early days were happy days for all of us, but a whole new world of responsibilities was looming.

When baby number two was on the way the two bedroomed prefab was no longer big enough. Mum knew the signs and, although she was a bit upset, she was a kind old soul and before long she was scheming with Sylvia as to how she could help us. "I'll make you some cot blankets and we'll have to see about finding you a place of your own to live."

In a relatively short time number 49 Redhill Avenue, Glasshoughton, a small house in a mining community with a pit and some coke ovens, became our new home. Our little house was right at the top of a hill which meant we had to climb up a lot of steps from Front Street, the main road, then left past the Glasshoughton Junior and Mixed Infants School, up the narrow one way street which was Redhill Avenue to the top opposite Brookes' shop before we reached it. It was one in a row of four terraced houses in a small yard.

We bought the house through an arrangement with the previous owner who had originally owned the whole row. We were able to do this after agreeing to put down a deposit of £50 and pay the rest at £2 per week. The total cost was to be £275. Although this doesn't sound much by today's standards, neither was my wage which, even with overtime included, was only £11 per week and Sylvia had given up work when Stephen was born.

The toilets were at the end of the yard and the bath hung at the back of the pantry door. Although it was wired for electricity, until the electricity board came and passed it, we were stuck with the gas lights and cold water. When I hear people discussing their daughter's or their son's impending weddings, "They've got everything, wall to wall carpets, fitted wardrobes, washing machine, television, double glazing," I think back to those days when my brother Les went with us to Brown Brothers and Taylor's, the local furniture shop, where we ordered a three piece suite, a carpet and a dining room suite and agreed to pay two pounds a week, a commitment which frightened me to death. My mother and Sylvia went to an auction at a pub to buy our kitchen equipment. The double bed and wardrobe my parents gave us, and the peggy tub and mangle were handed down by grandparents as a wedding present. But for all that we were very grateful to everybody for everything.

Our first night living in the new house was hair raising. The night started ordinarily enough. The electricity wasn't yet connected so I stood on the stool to turn out the gas light in the living room then we went up the stairs carrying a candle in a holder. I lit the gas bracket on the wall in the bedroom, Sylvia settled the baby down in the cot and then I turned the gas out, keeping a torch at the side of the bed for emergencies. After a while we got off to sleep, then suddenly in the early hours of the morning we were wakened by this terrific rumbling sound that seemed to go on for ever, followed by the smell of soot. I sat up shaking. Sylvia rushed to the baby.

"What the bloody hell was that?" I said.

Sylvia, just as scared, said, "I don't know."

Clutching the torch I plucked up courage to open the bedroom door; I don't know what I expected to find, maybe that the stairs wouldn't be there! The smell of soot became stronger but the stairs were still there so I pretended to be brave and went downstairs with Sylvia close behind me. As we got to the bottom step, the smell of soot was even stronger. I walked through the little kitchen into the living room, shining the torch nervously round the room. As the torch shone on the hearth and new carpet I stopped dead in my tracks.

"Bloody hell," I said. "The chimney's only fallen in."

Lying on the carpet was a big pile of soot and chimney bricks. What a mess! By the time I'd cleaned up the worst of it, it was daylight so I went round to our neighbour and explained what had happened. Bernard Blackburn was an ambulance driver who was trained to be sympathetic.

"I thought I'd heard something," he said.

I explained that we had a vacuum cleaner but no electricity so he agreed to lend me his hand pushed carpet sweeper. We had made ourselves known to our neighbours!

Bernard's wife, Mary, was expecting their first child a month after our second was due and they lived at the end house in the row. They were young like us so we got to know them very well after that; their Janet and our Wendy became good playmates as they got older.

Bernard was a motorbike enthusiast and he bought a motorbike and sidecar. They used to go off on little trips in the summer so I eventually got one myself and he was a great help showing me how to maintain it. My first sidecar looked more like the cockpit of an aircraft so I decided to build another. During the winter nights I set to and built a huge sidecar in the living room. When finished it looked more presentable than the old one but when it was time for me to take it outside, it wouldn't go through the door. I had to dismantle the top part and reassemble it when I got it outside.

That motorbike and sidecar came in very useful. As we didn't have a washing machine, we would pile all the washing on top of Sylvia and the two children in the sidecar and take it up to my mother's at Normanton. There Sylvia would wash and spin dry the clothes that she couldn't do by hand at home.

During the first weekend in January 1957 we visited Sylvia's Uncle Sam at The Cross Keys at Snydale. We met my sister, Bessie, there for a drink. During the evening, Sylvia went into the first stages of labour with Michael. It was late and Bessie insisted that we stayed the night at her house in Normanton in view of Sylvia's condition. It was the right decision because Michael was born early the next morning on the 6th January, eighteen months after Wendy. Having just celebrated Christmas and New Year, Sylvia remembered that we had not taken the trimmings down and that it was unlucky if you left them up after twelfth night. I went all the way back to Glasshoughton to take them down.

Bessie could always be relied on and she and Sylvia became great friends who shared the same sense of humour. Bessie also had a young family to bring up. Her husband Percy worked away for months at a time so we were able to support her when she needed it.

The painting trade wasn't a very reliable job and when Christmas came round many painters would be laid off because of the bad weather. Having three children to support now, I decided to put away my paint brush and look for other work. I found a more reliable all year round job on the buses. It was hard going.

We had a relation through marriage who was a master farrier. When he and his wife, who had no children, visited strangers, he would say, 'This is my wife Daisy, and she's barren you know.'

What an attitude. By the same token when I introduced my wife I should have said, 'This is my wife Sylvia, and she's highly fertile!'

We had seven children in eight years, four girls and three boys.

*

It was just before Christmas 1956 when I started my new job as a bus conductor. It was the kind of job where you met people, greeted them and felt as though you were in charge. Plenty of overtime provided a good living, and working split shifts gave me time to help Sylvia with the family and time to get to grips with a wonderful, zany neighbourhood.

Living on Redhill Avenue was an experience that all couples should have. Although we didn't have much money in those days and were restricted with our large family, we made our own fun with friends and neighbours and organised parties at the least of excuses. In the end though, family size made us move on. Our little two up and two down was no longer big enough. We started to look for something larger but in the end it was the Council who helped us make a decision. Our house and the rest of Redhill Avenue came under a Compulsory Purchase Order and we were all to be rehoused locally. Then Lady Luck shone on us again. We were given a house just round the corner on The Croft, a large family house with three big bedrooms and a front room, a bathroom with hot water and, most importantly, room for a piano, a piano to sing around.

Working on the buses meant that one week I worked alternate shifts; the early shift, starting at four thirty in the morning, and the late shift the following week, finishing around eleven forty-five. This was a regular pattern so busmen and women missed out on the social side of life when working late. To compensate, the crews organised their own social evenings in private rooms in public houses. Wives and husbands were invited providing, in our case, that baby sitters were available. Many of the occasions were to raise funds for the children's treats. Our growing family benefited from those.

It was on one of these occasions I teamed up with Derek Varley, a bus conductor who played guitar. We got on together and got a few numbers off and did one or two local charity shows under the names of Steve and Alan. This professional name came from the first two names of my eldest boy. Show business, I now realise, came to our home early. When the two of us rehearsed at our house, the children used to pop their heads through the serving hatch and take it all in. By the time we had finished rehearsing they also were word perfect and in tune with all our songs. It was because of this they got interested and I decided to teach them a song called Who Killed Cock Robin. Each had a different part like the sparrow, the owl, the rook and the fly and as they sang the final chorus they carried the youngest, Glyn, shoulder-high like pall bearers, with Judith holding a prayer book and leading the procession. Even then I knew that my children were able to learn songs quickly and, most of all, to perform without any nerves. Confirmation of their ability also came from another source.

The bus company used to run trips to the seaside every year, a smashing day out for the families. Committee members would argue amongst themselves as to which two would travel on the bus with the Poole family, they knew they were going to be well entertained on the way. Once when we were going to Filey and the kids were singing as usual, the bus driver was so engrossed with their singing of The Happy Wanderer that he drove completely round a roundabout and had to come off at the next exit.

They were forever singing. When it was my Sunday off, Sylvia and I took the kids over to Grandma and Grandad Poole's house in Normanton. We'd have lunch and afterwards the children always sang. They were wonderful family occasions.

Grandma used to say to Angela, "Where's my little star?" This was Angela's cue to sing a song called Like I Do. The tune was perfect but, since Angela made up her own words, the phrase that came over clearest was 'like a star'. That's why Grandma gave her the name of 'my little star'.

On Judith's turn, my brother Les would say, "Pass the microphone," handing her the chrome poker from the fireside, and Judith would do a perfect take-off of Cilla Black singing Anyone Who Had a Heart.

That's how it went. Each of the kids said a nursery rhyme or sang a song or danced; even in those early days you could sense some sort of magic in them.

My partner Derek was a member of the Magic Circle and often performed tricks for the children. I was visiting Derek at his home one day - he was on bed rest because he had an ulcerated leg - and I took four year old Glyn with me. Derek's mother made us both welcome and, as she gave me a cup of tea, she asked Glyn would he like some sweets?

"I bet he will sing you a song for one," I said, and with that I picked him up and sat him on top of the huge mantle shelf. Glyn sang The Wedding from beginning to end, word perfect and in tune. When he had finished I had a lump in my throat and there were tears in the old lady's eyes. She gave him the whole bag of sweets.

Eventually Derek and I invested in the act. We bought ourselves some decent sound equipment comprising of an amplifier with built-in echo or reverb, together with mike and stand. Now Derek was able to plug in his guitar and this gave us a full, all round sound. With this sort of set up we became quite popular on the club circuit. On one occasion we were the supporting act to Ken Kirkham from the BBC Northern Dance Orchestra. For this show we were paid £12, almost a week's wages on the buses. For that we did two twenty minute spots.

With that under our belt I began to think we had really made it, especially when we managed to get an audition with the Joseph Brothers at the famous City Varieties in Leeds. It was on a Tuesday morning and we were on the late shift, so we were able to go without interfering with work. A friend of ours, who was a bus driver on the same shift, offered to take us. Melvin was a quiet sort of a lad, always interested in our showbiz escapades and he had taken us to some of our club venues in his car. Neither Derek or myself could drive, so we were glad to pay him expenses. He reckoned to be a sort of manager, he kept a diary and he used to talk to the concert secretaries and organise any further engagements for us.

Our visit to the City Varieties in Leeds coincided with the Merrion Centre being built and when we arrived in Leeds we found that all the roads in the area were under construction. Melvin parked his car as near as he could but it was still a long way from the theatre. I had thought we might have this problem beforehand and so I had made a trolley out of wood with four small wheels and a long handle. We strapped the amplifier on and set off across the city. We must have looked funny wheeling this valuable piece of equipment through the centre of Leeds but I was so busy thinking, "I wonder if people know that we are future stars?"

I soon found out when we were called on stage to do our bit for the Josephs. Someone shouted, "Next!" and we walked out in front of Stanley Joseph, his brother Michael and a few more agents. We went straight into our first number, Walk Tall, a song Val Doonican had a hit with at the time. Then I sang You'll Never Walk Alone. That was it.

Michael Joseph shouted up, "Okay. Leave your card with Wally the stage manager. Next!"

We hurried off stage and packed up, feeling very deflated. We never did hear anything from them and we put it down to experience.

Not long after that I suspected that Derek was losing interest. When I took him to task about it he told me he had found a lady friend who happened to be married. It came out that she wanted him to break up our partnership and go solo with her as his manager and she made it obvious that I didn't fit in with their future plans.

In some respect I was glad to make the break. I decided to have a crack at going solo myself, but it wasn't the same, even though I got some good engagements. I still needed someone else to work with. Eventually I got a booking in Selby where the trio backing me were looking for a front man. I teamed up with the drummer and the lead guitarist and we called ourselves 'The Steve Alan Combo' but, after doing the local circuit for a

CYRIL + HEDLEY? ALAN (DRUMMER)

15

while with a certain amount of success, we became a bit stale and decided to go our separate ways.

*

The children attended the Pontefract Road Methodist Chapel on Smawthorne Lane. The minister, John McCarthy, introduced a new form of worship into this Chapel, in the form of guitar accompaniment for his family service. From the youngsters in the congregation he formed a little group called 'Bar Six' and the children became key members. Wendy played guitar along with Mr McCarthy and Stephen, Michael, Angela and Judith provided the vocals. This group often visited the residents of Castleford's old people's homes and led the hymn singing.

Once I'd packed in the entertainment business it was back to normal with family life, enjoying school days with the children and watching them grow up and develop into individuals in their own right.

We hadn't planned for a family of seven in the first place, but as each one arrived, they brought a special kind of love which is hard to describe. Toys and clothes were handed down and, if Sylvia made dresses for the girls, they were made from yards and yards of the same material to get as many dresses out of one piece as she could. Meal times were on the same principle, heads down and tuck in to whatever she concocted. I suppose the teachers in Glasshoughton School probably saw them more as individuals, just having one of our family in a class at a time, but we didn't have that luxury. When we spoke about them we referred to them as 'the boys' or 'the girls' or 'the kids'. Of course, they knew each other as individuals but also as members of a group. When the need arose though they could act in unison with quite sophisticated results.

The Sunday School teacher, Mavis, also played the piano. They liked her but this didn't mean they wouldn't have a bit of fun at her expense. When she turned round to play a hymn, like clockwork our children would lead other kids and get them to quietly switch the movable back rest of the long seat to the front. When Mavis turned round they were all facing the other way. Another stunt that they frequently pulled on poor Mavis came at the end of the lesson. She would say, "Close your hymn books," and the kids, who must have rehearsed this to perfection, each closed their books a split second after one another. The result sounded something like machine gun fire.

That's the sort of collective activity that my children were capable of.

Pranks really, but good training for people who were going to have a stage career.

Sylvia was a very caring mother who knew every mood of the children and involved herself in all of their activities at home or at school. They brought her out and gradually she changed from the shy young girl I had married into a very impressive woman. She always had a laugh and a joke with everyone but was also dependable and a good organiser. She didn't lose any of her good looks: her bright eyes and her rosy cheeks that never needed make-up. There was no mistaking who the children took after. She recognised the importance of being active in the neighbourhood, at chapel and at school.

I was very aware, at this stage, that Sylvia needed a break from baby-talk, so I insisted every week that she should have her hair done at the hairdressers. She was a bit reluctant at first so I went down to the hairdressers on Front Street and made an appointment for her. This was to prove to be the beginning of a new lease of life for Sylvia because being tied down with the children she used to look forward to her weekly meetings at the salon. At Christmas time the customers would take mince pies and cake to the shop and share a bottle of wine; the salon became more of a community meeting place. Betty Broxup was the hairdresser and she made Sylvia very welcome and they became good friends. Occasionally when we could get baby sitters we went out for a meal with Betty and her husband, Ted. Sometimes we took the children to their house for tea. I used to say to them that it was like entertaining a bus party. Not everybody would take on the task of inviting a family of our size but they and their two children enjoyed having us there.

When the June Summer Fayre came round, Sylvia always made seven little aprons for the kids to take to sell on the school stall. Each year the teachers would say to them, 'Please ask your mam to get the sewing machine cracking,' and she did. It was a lovely neighbourhood school and we owe it a lot. Mrs Jackson was the Head of the Infants and she introduced all our children to the first stages of education. When she retired, Mr Wright the Headmaster invited our family to sing for her. It was all kept secret to surprise her, so you can imagine the feelings that came across at that performance. Mrs Jackson was in tears.

Seven little Pooles

The family that plays together, stays together

Chapter Two

It was late one October evening in 1965. Our local grocer, Ted Brookes, and his wife Joan called round. Ted, a tall chap with a small moustache, had the corner shop at the top of Redhill Avenue. All the kids from Glasshoughton Juniors knew Ted because he'd exchanged banter with them when they called to buy sweets after school. Both Joan and Ted had the patience of Job, as a shop keeper must who sells sweets at a penny a time and watches each child deliberate over their choice. I liked them from the first. Ted did all the talking and Joan just butted in to correct him. They had come to ask if I would be a guest at the Methodist Chapel concert. I had sung there the previous year with my old partner Derek, but I had to tell them that we didn't sing together any more. I was eager to help but who was going to accompany me? Joan suggested that the children should sing with me. She put in motion a train of events which was to lead well beyond any experience I could have imagined.

She said she would ask the Chapel organist, Les Smalley, to accompany us. I knew Les. He had been brought up in the Methodist Chapel all his life and his father had been a preacher on the local circuit. On first appearances he seemed rather straight-laced. Asking him to play was a little bit like asking a vicar, but when I got to know him he was not as he had seemed. Quite the contrary.

After next to no discussion he agreed to rehearse with us and provide the accompaniment at the concert. What should we sing? Then I had an idea based on something that had happened a few months earlier. I had come home from work one Sunday to find all my children in the room round the piano. Wendy was pinging out notes from a sheet of music. To the familiar sound of Do-Re-Mi I found them each engrossed in singing their own little part. When I looked closer, I found that they had the music from the film The Sound of Music.

"Where have you got that from?" I enquired, surprised at seeing it.

"Oh, we've been to Bev and Kathleen's and they said we could have it," answered Wendy.

"Bev and Kathleen who used to live at the back of us at Redhill Avenue?" I said.

They all nodded in a sheepish manner.

"But when did you go to their house?" I asked, knowing full well that they were supposed to have gone to Sunday School. Stephen then began to explain, "We went that way to Sunday School and as we were passing their house our Wendy said shall we call."

Wendy butted in here, "Yes, and we were all singing and we forgot about the time for Sunday School until it was too late to go."

I stared rather hard at them and said, "So you mean you haven't been?"

They all looked rather red-faced and shook their heads.

"But we can sing most of the songs," Michael piped up. At this, they all looked at me for some sort of approval.

I said, "I'm glad you can but you shouldn't have missed Sunday School. I don't know what Mr McCarthy will think of you."

At that point Sylvia came into the room.

"The tea is ready," she said. "Have they told you where they've been?"

"Oh, yes," I replied, "but I have told them they must not do it again."

That copy of music which Bev Ward and his wife Kathleen gave them is the one from which they did their very first concert and it is cherished by us to this day. Little did they know what they helped to spark off from that musical Sunday afternoon. Bev and Kathleen were very proud of the children and watched whenever they appeared on the television.

We managed to get together five songs from The Sound of Music and as this film conveniently featured a family of seven children of similar ages, we felt that the audience might relate to what they had seen on the silver screen.

When we had decided on the music then it was the choice of clothes. Sylvia decided on new dresses for the girls - this was the proud mum coming out - and new shirts for the boys. I also made a suggestion, "What about making them some dicky bows and cummerbunds? We've got some nice red material we could use."

*

On the night of the concert, Wendy came to me with tears in her eyes and said, "Our Judith's locked herself in the toilet."

I went back stage into the ladies, climbed over the top of the door and there was poor Judith with tears like bob taws. I dried her eyes and unlocked the door and assured her everything would be alright. We were all a bit nervous but when the children came out on stage, nobody would have guessed what had taken place just before. Sylvia sat at the piano with Les and turned the pages when appropriate. It was down to us.

The kids opened with the title song from The Sound of Music and I joined them half way through to finish the number. This got us all on stage together and, to our delight, it had the desired effect of bringing spontaneous applause from our audience. We followed with My Favourite Things, Maria, Do-Re-Mi. When little Glyn stepped forward to sing his part you could feel the atmosphere; he was only four. We completed our spot with the full hall joining in with Edelweiss.

After the show people crowded round to tell us how much they had enjoyed it and ask why we didn't do more of the same. This was a whole new experience for us and we savoured the moment.

Before long we were inundated from near and far with requests to perform for all kinds of churches, chapels and charities. We decided that the show in its present form was not going to be enough and that we'd have to get our thinking caps on if we were to fulfil our obligations.

'Uncle' Les Smalley, as he was called by the children, said that he was interested enough to take on the task of permanent accompanist.

"I would have been very upset if you hadn't asked me," he said, delighted at the chance. Ted Brookes, our grocer friend, agreed to help us knock the show together, so everything was in place.

A typical two hour show went something like this. Ted linked the opening musical selections by telling a few clean jokes and then introduced the Poole Family. After each selection he would clap us off, telling a few more jokes and then bring us on again. Our repertoire included songs from Hans Christian Andersen, Mary Poppins, Pinocchio and popular songs from other shows. Sylvia was very good at harmony and she was roped in to sing. Although she was a very shy person she became very enthusiastic and proved to be very valuable to the act. To complete it all, Les Smalley's wife Eve and Joan Brookes were wardrobe mistresses.

Yet it wasn't all sweetness and light. The children always gave their best on stage, but behind the scenes they had their fights over the colour of Opal Fruit they wanted or who should sing which song.

After a few months, concerts came so thick and fast that we had to limit performances to only two a week. We would have little meetings as letters requesting our services came in and we had to plan well in advance. Les Smalley was a council committee clerk so we had to avoid the first Thursday and the third Thursday in the month. I was working alternate shifts so unless I had an early finish or could change a shift, that also caused complications. That December we had the pleasure of being asked to perform at the Christmas party organised for the bus workers. This meant doing two shows, one when my shift was working earlies, and one the following week when the opposite shift was working earlies. These parties were always held at the Kiosk dance hall in Castleford and I felt proud to be able to present my family there. But for all that, it was time for a change. One Thursday I happened to see an advert in the local paper requiring a warehouse man for Marks and Spencer's in Castleford. This meant regular day work. In June 1966 I applied and got the job. I was sad to be leaving all my colleagues on the buses but they all wished me well and I still keep in touch with many of them.

Being a day worker meant that I could call round at the Music Centre in Castleford and order new copies of the music we needed to keep abreast of the changing music scene. I got on friendly terms with Ken Dando, the owner of the shop, and he became very interested in our work. Things were going well when out of the blue a young lady from the local Pontefract and Castleford Express said she had heard about our work for charity and that she would like to do a feature on us. Pictures were arranged for the following day during my dinner hour. Dressed in my best suit with all the children dressed in the clothes they used for singing, we stood around our large round table and sang. I remember the table well because it was very sturdy and just right for a family of our size. I had acquired it from a friend of ours, the local undertaker, Eddie Ashton, whose wife Iris was a teacher at Glasshoughton School - she had taught our children when they passed through her class. She had asked me to paint their living room and the table had been in part payment. The family picture was in the paper the following Thursday. Not many people noticed the table, rather they concentrated on the full page spread and a very good write up. It also compared us with the Von Trapp Family Singers, the family in the film The Sound of Music.

After this our popularity grew even more quickly. On one of my visits to Ken Dando's shop he mentioned that he supplied organs to Yorkshire Television and that Jess Yates was doing a new children's show called Junior Showtime.

"I have told him all about you and I'm sure he's interested," he said.

In some ways it was a throw-away line and I didn't give Ken's comments a lot of thought. People say all sorts of things that rarely materialise, so we carried on with our concerts and, although I mentioned it to family and friends hoping for the best, it went no further. I was surprised then when one Tuesday morning, early in 1969, as I was busy in the store, in walked Ken Dando with a big grin on his face.

"Cyril, get the family organised for tonight," he said. "Jess has just rung up and he would like you to go over to the studios for 7.30."

I was gobsmacked. At dinner time I nipped home and told Sylvia. From there it was all systems go. First I ran up to see Ted to ask if he could drive us there. Then Ted rang Les at the Town Hall to see if he was free. Ken didn't know what a complicated machine he had set in motion. Both Ted and Les said "Yes", so we were all set to make our first visit to the Yorkshire Television studios in Leeds.

At that time the studios were not finished, but they still seemed very big to us. We managed to park with the assistance of one of the security men, then we approached the reception desk and told the lady who we had come to see. To her it was routine.

"Oh yes," she said. "Mr Yates isn't in yet but he said I was to take you into the canteen and he will see you there."

We went through some massive double doors and into an enormous canteen filled with people. Some looked like office staff, others were in trendy clothes and there were the 'over here darlings' who spoke in loud voices so that everyone could hear. We found out later they were scene shifters. We had entered a new world. Me and Ted went and ordered some teas, little knowing that this was going to be the pattern of our lives for the next few years.

We seemed to be there for hours and I was beginning to think that we had been forgotten when suddenly a huge, round-faced chap with a big hat and glasses came through the door. He marched straight up to our table. Mr Jess Yates had arrived. We soon found out that it was almost impossible to get a word in edgeways. He was the one who did all the talking.

"Hello kids. I know all about you."

I tried to butt in, "Er, we've been here ages."

"Yes, well if you will come early. I'm a very busy man. I have two shows on the go and they are fully networked. We have millions of viewers," he went on.

While he was talking he set off through another door at the other end of the canteen and we all followed like a flock of sheep. He was still talking as he opened the lift door and guided us into the biggest lift we had ever seen. "This," he said, "is a Poole Family size lift."

We all laughed. We were supposed to. He then said, "Wait while they all see you lot on the box!" This wasn't at all like being at a Joseph Brothers audition at the City Varieties. He had energy.

When we arrived at the right floor the door opened and he whisked us off down the corridor and into a room with a piano. There he introduced us to the director of Junior Showtime, David Mallet.

"Hello Mr Poole and hello Mrs Poole," said this very professional young man. "We've heard so much about you and your family."

Quickly Jess Yates introduced us to a young woman standing with pen and paper at the ready. "This is Jenny Everett. She's my secretary and also my personal assistant when I'm producing."

"Hello," she said in a friendly voice.

"Who is the pianist?" Jess asked.

I thought poor old Les was going to die on the spot, he was so worked up. But he stepped forward to take his seat at the piano with Sylvia close behind him to give him confidence.

"Okay, kids," said Jess Yates. "Let's hear what you can do."

The kids started singing an excerpt from The Sound of Music. I joined in but I instinctively knew he wasn't interested in me. In fact, I thought he wasn't very interested in any of it. He was gabbling away to the director and to his secretary.

"He's not bloody listening!" I said to Ted.

After a while Les stopped playing, he had run out of music. I quickly passed him some more copies.

"Come on, do some more," Jess said. Then he carried on just the same as before. The kids were singing their hearts out and he wasn't listening. I couldn't grasp what was going on.

Then he stood up, everything stopped, and he walked over to me and Sylvia.

"That's alright," he said. "Now then, I want Glyn to be Pinocchio and I want all the rest to be dressed in period costume. We will have some specially made. I have also got some of the clothes from the film Oliver. We can use some of those too. Now then, how about licences? You will have to get them sorted out."

He told us the name of the Chief of Education for the West Riding and gave us some forms. "You'll have to make an appointment to see him. It's all been changed, you see." With that, he exited as quickly as he had arrived.

*

Getting the licences was less trouble than I had expected but they were complicated. The licences governed the number of performances each of our children could give a year, depending on their ages. We were only allowed forty performances a year for each child under twelve, and eighty for those over twelve. We had to sort out our priorities. On our large list of things to do, teaching the children new songs was the top. Quickly we had to have in place a duet for Denise and Glyn, No Two People Have Ever Been So In Love from Hans Christian Andersen. Uncle Les Smalley worked very hard with them and in no time at all it was perfect. It was fortunate that they learned new songs quickly because, as we were very soon to find out, in many cases we got the scripts one day and were on the set the next.

Glyn's script would arrive by Monday's post. Only then would we discover that the family were to take part too. Each week the show had a different theme and required the kids to learn different songs. One week the theme might be 'by the seaside' and the kids would have to learn songs like By the Sea and I Scream, You Scream, We All Scream For Ice Cream.

The sets were all very colourful. An actor called Bobby Bennet fronted the show with Glyn and a puppet called Mr Albert. Bobby and Glyn sometimes portrayed characters from fairy stories like Pinocchio. For this Bobby played Geppetto, the old wood carver, and Glyn dressed like a puppet and sang I've Got No Strings. It was exhausting. Sylvia had to take the kids at least three times a week to the Yorkshire Television studios for rehearsals. Jess did two shows per recording, so every other Sunday we would go to the City Varieties to do this. There were people everywhere; stage hands, cameramen, electricians, technicians, sound men, lighting men and then all the kids who were taking part plus their parents. As part of the operation they had removed half of the seating down one side to make room for everyone.

The morning was spent at camera rehearsals. The floor manager, wearing earphones called cans, controlled the whole thing. He would shout, "Quiet please! Studio. Cue music. Ten seconds on the clock. Start the clock." A stage hand held a clapper board with a clock on it in front of the camera as the seconds ticked away, then you would hear the Junior Showtime introduction. On getting this cue the floor manager would hold up his hands and, as the clock pointed to the last second, he would drop his arm and point it to Bobby Bennet. Bobby would then begin to say his opening lines to the camera. Stopping and starting they would go on lining up each part of the show.

It was new to us, but we could understand it all. The floor manager was receiving his instructions from the director, high up above the studio in the control room. Everybody who was taking part had to be in the right place at the right time and on the correct camera. This meant that the show had to be scripted for each cameraman. There were four cameras, one very high up in the gallery, so it was a very complicated procedure. When the director and floor manager were satisfied they had been through all the shots for both shows, the lights would go up and the floor manager would inform us that the first show would take place at five o'clock prompt.

That was the cue for the family machine to move into operation as Sylvia made sure the kids got their packed lunch in the old theatre bar. I went off to the cashier in the next room to get our expenses. The long queue usually moved pretty fast. Each child was paid £3 expenses each, and we were at the theatre from eight in the morning until six o'clock at night.

This happened many times but you just remember the best, like this occasion. Just before it was time to go back into the theatre Jess came in to see us.

"I've been watching the kids on the monitor,' he said, 'and I think they look a bit too serious. I've had a word with the floor manager and I would like you, Sylvia, to go down and sit underneath Camera One and get the buggers to smile. They'll do anything for you and besides it will help if they see a face they know. What I'd like you to do is smile at the kids, but at the same time do this." Then, with his index finger, he made several circular motions round his mouth to emphasise his smile.

This operation became a standing joke for years. The kids would say, "We've got the only mother who, instead of getting on the camera, gets underneath it."

Back in the theatre they were letting kids into the seats. The audience came from Yorkshire schools and, as they were ushered to their places, they were each given a stick of rock lettered right through with the words Junior Showtime together with streamers and paper hats. When they were all in place, Jess came out in front of them with his large hat on and started to tell them that although they were the audience, they were part of the show.

"That camera will be on you for audience reaction shots, so when you see this hat waving in the air, I want you to clap and cheer as loud as you can. When I put it on my head and start to laugh, I want you to laugh. Do that or I'll take the rock off you!"

He was a professional and after a few demonstrations he had them in fits of laughter. That over, the lights went down and the floor manager took over.

At the first recording everything began well. Bobby and Glyn introduced all kinds of acts from all parts of the country and then it was the Poole Family. Sylvia and I sat in the celebrity box at the side of the stage and we had the privilege of being introduced to the viewers. Then there was a major hitch, a power cut. It was the outside broadcasting units that had a power failure and everything went off. Jess Yates was unflappable. He took Glyn on his lap and sat down on the stage in front of all the children.

"This is Glyn," he said, "and he is only seven years old. Under the new laws he is the youngest ever to appear on television."

All the children cheered. He carried on nursing Glyn and explained to the children what was going on. Eventually the lights came on again and the show was completed.

Under normal circumstances we would have only had to wait until the following Tuesday to see our first appearance on the show on television, but the previous weekend there had been a violent storm and the Emley Moor transmitting tower had been blown down. This meant we had to wait another fortnight until a temporary mast could be erected.

Jess had done a good job on publicity, the papers were full of photographs and stories about the Poole Family. He also had another angle to work on - that Glyn was the youngest star ever to appear legally on television.

The press releases and the very fact that our family was something new on television meant that Jess got lots of letters asking if the Poole Family could open garden parties or charity galas. Sylvia and the kids did their best to oblige by agreeing to attend them, but it was a lot of work. Most of the events were on a Saturday and this meant I had to work, but Ted managed to get away from the shop and he took them while his wife Joan and I carried on working.

These little excursions had their moments though. One particular garden party they opened was at Rodley in Leeds. Jess asked Sylvia to take the kids to wardrobe at the studios. We had some tartan kilts made for the children for one of the shows and he thought it would be a good idea for them to wear them at the gala. Well, this almost started World War III. The boys didn't want to be seen wearing frocks. Michael hid somewhere and almost made them late for the event, then Stephen was adamant that if the others weren't going to wear them, he wasn't either. I still don't know how they got round it, but they finally opened the gala in the kilts. What I do know though is that I have never seen any pictures of them in kilts. No photos was part of the deal.

Early publicity shot

Chapter Three

Bobby Bennet's marriage to Jenny Everett (Jess Yates' secretary) was a YTV spectacular. Jess played the church organ and we sang. The children stood at the front of the church in a little group formation and sang I Believe. Stephen was at the back left with Angela and Denise in front of him but both slightly angling to his left, and Wendy back right, with Michael and Judith in front of her, angling to her right. This made a V formation down to where Glyn stood.

The reception was at the Parkways Hotel and nothing was spared. This was the first time I'd ever tasted real champagne and that afternoon Jess - we had by this time dropped the Mr Yates - started a conversation which was to alter all our lives. He had been offered the task of producing a new show for television, a semi-religious programme for early Sunday evenings aimed at the people who would like to go to church but, for some reason or another, were not able to go.

He said, "I thought the kids sang very well in church this afternoon. That was the first time you have heard me play. Well, I'm going to play on this new programme and I was thinking in church, wouldn't it be nice to have a regular spot for your children. Do you think they would do it?"

Sylvia and I both looked at one another and then Sylvia said, "Our children first started singing in church. I'm sure they will be delighted at the chance."

"The programme will be fully networked," Jess went on. "It will be showing in all the regions of ITV, not only Yorkshire. I have been given six shows to test for public reaction."

We got some measure of the show when Ted and Les, armed with hymn books, put up ideas and Jess started saying things like,

"This will do for Harry Secombe, and this will be alright for Moira Anderson, but of course we will have to sort something out for Maggie Fitzgibbons." She was in a popular soap called The Newcomers at the time. It was all very exhausting but nice to think we were in right at the beginning of the show.

Stars on Sunday was launched with Harry Secombe, Moira Anderson and Liz Fox, a popular news presenter from Yorkshire TV to give a local flavour, as the main people. Our children, because of requests, had a spot in every alternate show. Yet for all the systematic thought that went into it, Jess knew how to exploit an accident. Once when we were doing one of the recordings, a cat came on to the set from out of the scenery dock next door. It climbed up the stairs where the children sat and began to move from one to the other. It looked so natural and comfortable that the director decided to keep it in shot. It looked funny because when it opened its mouth it looked as though it was singing. The kids loved it and nicknamed it Sos, after the first letters of the words Stars on Sunday.

Jess, as he had promised, played the organ and, although he used to steam roller through the music at a fast rate, when playing for our children it proved to be very popular with the viewers.

The format of the show was pretty simple. Liz Fox introduced the main people and read out the letters of request from viewers. Part of the programme was dedicated to favourite passages from the Bible. These were also requested. Film stars, members of the clergy from all denominations including the Archbishop of Canterbury, and also some members of the royal family all got involved at this stage.

This new show really took off and the big stars were queuing up to take part. Because our children were on pretty regularly, their popularity grew and the requests really started flooding in. Everywhere we went we had packed houses, but we still did our share of village halls and, no matter how small the organisations, we tried our best to help them out but we were now able to pick and choose. The legal situation with the licenses meant that we could use the restrictions to protect the children from doing too many programmes. We had some wonderful times.

We had been invited to the village hall at Hensall, near Goole. As usual the people had kindly sent us directions but somehow we had come in at the wrong end of the village. We were driving along when we came across some people carrying chairs. I leaned out of the window and asked, 'Could you tell me the way to the village hall?'

This chap shouted back in a very country accent, "Yes, just foller us. It's just raandt corner. Err ave yer browt summet ter sit on? We've browt arr owen chairs cosst Poole Family's on toneet." That was great.

Performing on television also introduced us to new friends like the Doncaster Wheatsheaf Girls' Choir and we were invited to take part in some of their live concerts. Jess had lots of local talent in his show, the Salvation Army, the York Celebration Choir, Bev Jones and the York Singers, the West Yorkshire Police Choir Band. There were various operatic societies and the Gott Sisters who were two wonderfully talented teenage pianists from Harrogate. We performed with all these people.

And what hospitality we experienced. When we arrived at Allerton Bywater they asked us the title of our last number before the interval because the fish and chip shop across the road needed to know when to cook our supper. Sure enough, when we came off stage at the interval, on the table was fish and chips for all of us. We all climbed back on stage feeling very fat and very full.

At another chapel poor old Les had to stand up and say, "I'm very sorry ladies and gentlemen, but we can't possibly do our programme with this piano." The poor woman who had organised the show was virtually in tears, but after a long discussion with her and another gentleman who owned a piano, we arranged to go back the following week. The place was packed. Yet for all this new work we tried not to lose sight of old friends.

The children still attended Sunday school and one Sunday John McCarthy and his wife Maureen asked us if they could take the children out to tea to John's Auntie Doris' house. It was her birthday and she had always wanted to meet the children. After tea they sang for her and John accompanied them on the guitar. Next day her next door neighbour said, "Excuse me asking, but was that the Poole Family who came to visit you on Sunday afternoon?"

"Yes," replied Auntie Doris, in a very proud voice.

"We thought it was," said the neighbour. "We were listening to them singing with our ears against the wall!"

Because the volume of requests for our live shows increased, I made a decision which at the time seemed right but which later on I regretted. I had seen an advert in the paper for Crown Topper hair pieces. I talked it over with Sylvia. My hair was gradually waving goodbye and I was on stage such a lot that we decided I should find out about them. Schofield's in Leeds had a salon upstairs where they were promoting hair pieces, so I decided to take a look there. On the bus journey into Leeds I still had doubts. I entered the salon as the consultant brushed the surplus hair from an elderly gentleman's shoulders and I thought, 'That's smart. You can't see the join.' My mind was made up.

The consultant settled me into a comfortable chair and several pieces of hair were tried for colour. With her expert help a suitable one was chosen before the process of fitting, cutting and styling began. It was wonderful. In what seemed to be no time at all I had a full head of hair, although I must admit that it felt as though I had a rug on my head. I was shown how to fix it securely with special tape which she assured me would make it perfectly safe in most conditions.

Now came the big test, my homeward journey. Sweat was already beginning to run down the back of my neck as I sat on the bus at Quarry Hill, but on the journey back nobody gave me a second glance. I got off the bus at Glasshoughton and walked up the lane to our house, still not meeting anybody I knew. So far so good. I was just about to open the garden gate when little Matthew Cartwright from across the road came running down the hill.

He glanced across at me very casually, as kids do, and shouted, "Hello Mr Poole. I like your new hair." I had come all the way from Leeds and this little lad, in paying me what he thought was a genuine compliment, had brought me down to earth.

I persevered and gradually the people around me began to accept it. People who didn't know me so well fortunately didn't even notice. With the wig firmly in place and a part of me, I didn't try to keep it a secret. I decided to treat it as a hat.

Now, not only were we performing regularly on television, but we were recording artists too - a new string to our bow. If only the grandparents had known what they had started all those years ago when they had encouraged us to sing. The love for music was definitely handed down from the two grandads. Grandad Charles, Sylvia's father, played cornet in the Sharlston Brass Band, and Grandad Poole had been a member of the Bing Boys, a group which sang for charity in local pubs and clubs around West Yorkshire just after the depression of the 1930s. Alas, poor Grandma and Grandad Poole didn't live long enough to see their grandchildren on television, although they did see their earlier performances at some of the local churches and chapels. Grandad Charles did. Although usually a reserved character, he loved it all.

"While we were on holiday in Blackpool, he had a queue of pensioners round him as he handed out the grandchildren's signed photographs. Bless him. Can you blame him for wanting to share in their bit of glory?" Grandma Charles once told Sylvia and me.

The family were always supportive but we owed a lot to Ted and Joan Brookes. We were a big family by any standards and if they hadn't run us about in their car and taken telephone calls, we would have found things very difficult.

Thanks also to Ted and Joan, we were able to have some lovely holidays. Ted's mother and his Auntie Flo owned two caravans at

Primrose Valley near Filey and, after Ted had talked to them, they let us have the use of one for a fortnight.

Auntie Flo said, "I'll move in with Ted's mother and you'll be able to come and we'll baby-sit for you some nights."

That was a wonderful offer and just what Sylvia and I needed. We were very grateful and we had lots of fun during the school summer holidays. Ted's two sons, Nigel and Clive, always came and joined us; Grandma and Auntie Flo made room for them in their caravan so there were always plenty for cricket. It was also sufficiently close for lots of our friends to come and visit us. Whenever we were on the beach we wrote 'The Pooles' in big letters on the sands so our friends could find us when they looked down from the cliff top. Even Jimmy Corrigan from Batley Varieties came to visit us there in his Rolls Royce. He just looked over the cliff and there we were.

It was on such a visit that I first realised that Les Smalley wasn't well. After he had made the high climb to the top of the cliff he looked dreadful and told us how he felt. We were very concerned and asked him to stay so he didn't have to drive home. I was glad to hear that he was well enough to go to work but knew that the pressure he was under was too great. He hadn't expected us all to go this far so we were not surprised when he decided to give up playing the piano for us. It was a reluctant decision and his doctor also advised him to take early retirement from his permanent job.

This was a big blow to us and we even thought about calling it a day ourselves, but we had lots of concerts in the pipeline. After a great deal of thought it was Les who finally made up our minds for us.

"Why don't you try to find someone else to play for you?" he asked. "I'm sure somebody who plays the organ or piano will be interested."

We had already considered this possibility. Basil Phillips was Mr Music in Featherstone. He was choirmaster for the Girnhill Singers at Girnhill Lane Club, musical director of Featherstone and District Amateur Musical and Dramatic Society and also accompanist for Featherstone and District Male Voice Choir at Wilson Street Chapel. Bas didn't realise how good he was. His musical capabilities were far in front of many who were in the business professionally. He was a down to earth family man who worked in the mining industry and when I watched his fingers flying up and down the keyboard I used to ask myself, "Why is this man risking those God-given fingers in industry?"

When you were with him he made you feel that your piece of music was the most important piece he had ever played and he made sure that the end product was perfect. So he was very approachable and I suppose this is why we felt able to ask him to help out.

Ted and Sylvia went to see him. Bas was eager to help and, after listening to him play, they agreed he was perfect.

Bas didn't take long to adapt to our type of entertainment and he also came up with some good ideas of his own. For instance, he introduced us to two more musicians. Jack Moulding was a bass player and Ian Glenn who, although only fifteen years old, was a very good drummer. So now we had our own trio to rehearse and play for us. That same year I passed my driving test and we bought a Transit van. We fitted it out with seats so we had enough room for us all to travel together. From the start everyone got on well together.

The first concert we did after Bas joined us, our children were on form, not only during the show but at the reception afterwards. The organisers had kindly baked some buns and when Basil wasn't looking each of the children ate a bun and then placed the bun papers in a pile on poor old Bas' plate. It was one way of saying welcome to the family!

We got all over the place in our Transit van. Once we went over to Cheshire to help out Les Smalley's son, Keith. It was a charity function organised by the Nantwich Lions.

When we got to our destination, a big farmhouse with acres of land, the lady of the house showed us into the dining room. The table was beautifully set out with all kinds of salads and meats when Ian, Stephen's friend, said over my shoulder, "There's only one thing on that table that I like, and it's bread." I felt like crawling into a mouse hole, but fortunately the lady pretended not to hear.

*

While working at Marks and Spencer's one of my early morning duties was to collect the mail and take it upstairs to the general office. One day to my surprise, amongst the letters was one postmarked Bristol with my name on it, care of the store. I felt obliged to open it. I found that it was from a man called Tony Hill, who explained in his letter he had read about the family in the papers. He was writing to ask if we would be able to put on a concert at a venue in Bristol.

I took the letter home and we had discussions about it, but decided that the journey would be too far and would mean the children losing time from school. Joan Brookes, who did all the correspondence for us, wrote back to him explaining the reasons why we wouldn't be able to come. This didn't seem to have any influence on him and two or three letters were exchanged with this very determined person. One of his suggestions was to charter a train and book us in at a large hotel in Bath. We thought that he must be a real impresario but we didn't change our minds.

Next we had a letter from him asking if he could come up and talk to us. Joan wrote back and said it would be alright but we still couldn't see the concert as being a viable proposition. We thought that this would be the end of the story but to our amazement one evening about half past ten when we arrived home from one of our concerts, outside the house was an old Ford Corsair and inside sat a very skinny young man. He introduced himself to us as Tony Hill from Bath. We asked him in and he explained that he had booked in at The Magnet pub just down the road. He appeared to be a nice lad and he told us, "I have a little printing business but I have always wanted to put on a big show for charity. I think that the Poole Family are the right sort of act to draw in the audience."

We again explained the difficulty in taking the show to Bristol and, that after taking out expenses, there might not be anything left for the charity. After a long discussion we compromised and agreed to do a show for him at the newly built Castleford Civic Centre. The idea was that he would do all the publicity and promotion and we would provide the show. We had sensed that not only was he a very determined young man, but also very genuine.

Tony suggested that the charity should have a local appeal. We told him that we had seen a request for donations by the Heart Foundation in Castleford and we contacted the organiser, Mr Dean of Airedale. He was delighted and said he would organise the sale of tickets. A date was firmly booked for December, 12th 1971. All we had to do was put the show together.

Jean Pearce, choreographer for Junior Showtime had often talked about joining in with us to do a show since we had helped her out with a similar venture, and so it was duly arranged. This was the first time I had been given the responsibility of organising a show of this size, but I took up the challenge and I enjoyed it. First of all I had to seek the services of people who would be responsible for the lighting. Then I needed someone for the sound. I was fortunate enough to meet a young man, John Dawson, who was a traffic policeman and had a good reputation for helping local dramatic societies with their productions. He built speakers and understood theatre lighting. His hobby could easily have been his profession.

Quickly we had a very professional show on the way. With Jean's talented crew, our own family, Bas and his trio, plus the help of John Dawson, how could we fail?

*

Castleford Showtime was a great success. Tony had done his job with the publicity. He had sent posters for us to put up and had printed the tickets. My job was to get all the artists to the show. It was arranged that I would drive over to Leeds at the last minute to pick up the dancers and then to over to Featherstone to pick up Bas. Everything was going well until we were on our way out of Leeds with the dancers and we discovered we had come without the girls' dresses. Panic set in.

"We'll just have to go back for them," I said, but when we got back to Jean's studio the door was locked. Time was getting short so we set off back to Castleford hoping that Jean would bring them.

Back at the Civic Centre the queue outside was really long; mums, dads and families were eager to get a good seat.

But I was late and someone else had to go for Bas. Fortunately I wasn't short of volunteers but we came unstuck directing this person to where I had arranged to pick up Bas. I went into the dressing room and found the girls' dresses had arrived, so that was one problem solved. I got myself ready. I was to open the show with a song I had written to the tune of Hello Dolly. The words introduced the different artists. I went to the back of the stage and found to my horror Bas hadn't arrived and it was time to start. Jean was also a pianist and said she would play for me until Bas arrived. Fortunately he turned up soon after the start.

As he settled down he said, "I never saw the minibus so when it got to ten to two I started walking and fortunately an old pal of mine came by and gave me a lift right to the door." That's a beauty of this area; people know each other and are always willing to help out.

The show was great but I learned one thing from the exercise - delegate, never try to do the whole thing yourself. If I was to put on another show I would be stricter with the artists when deciding how much time to allow them because we ran over schedule by an hour. Fortunately no-one minded and everyone said they had enjoyed the show. Our personal triumph was in filling the Civic Centre on a Sunday afternoon when normally most people would be coming out of the pubs. The Heart Foundation had their coffers topped up by around £300 and Tony Hill put on his dream show.

These days Tony runs his Cherished Number Plate Company and has also made a few appearances on television with his yellow Rolls Royce - whose number plate is MAD 1. We still keep in touch and often get together for a good laugh at the way we first met.

Glyn with Gracie Fields and other guest celebrities,
'Stars on Sunday' Christmas Special, 1972

Chapter Four

Our next television show was the biggest that Jess or Yorkshire Television had been asked to do. It was October 1972 and all the different television companies were preparing their Christmas shows. Jess had got the big one, a Stars on Sunday scheduled to go on the air on Christmas Day immediately before the Queen's speech. This was a peak viewing slot anyone would have been glad to have. To make it something special, he had talked Gracie Fields into coming out of retirement just for this show. Jess called the show Gift for Gracie and it was hosted by Lionel Blair. Gracie sang one of her most popular songs Bless This House and Glyn played a little Christmas tree elf who popped out of a large sack which Bruce Forsyth, as Santa, carried over his shoulder.

Bruce said, "Look at all those people enjoying themselves down there at Gracie's banquet."

To this cue Glyn replied, "And all that food. Isn't it boring just being a Christmas tree ornament, only being used once a year after they've blown that dust out of your ears and nostrils."

The other stars included stars of today like Les Dawson, Shirley Bassey and Harry Secombe, but also stars of yesterday such as Ted Ray, Sandy Powell and Arthur Askey. Towards the end, Glyn did a lovely song and dance with Gracie and the whole family were brought into the scene singing a selection of Christmas carols.

The show was a great success. Gracie thanked the children for taking part and presented them each with a Premium Bond, they cherish them to this day. Gracie is no longer with us but she will always be remembered for her kindness to our children. She told Glyn that she had been born the seventh in her family and hoped this would be a lucky omen for his future.

Just after the children had made the recording for Gift for Gracie, Sylvia had a phone call from The Sunday People asking if a reporter could come and interview her about the family. The man came one afternoon while I was at work and one of his questions was about the neighbours and their attitude to our family going out and giving concerts. Sylvia's answers were honest and to the point, every neighbour and person that we spoke to loved our children and nobody gave us anything but praise for what we were doing. That wasn't the answer he had wanted.

The following Sunday there was a photograph of the children peeping over our hedge and the header read People in Glasshoughton Should Not Throw Stones. It went on to give quotes from Sylvia alluding to the fact some of our neighbours were jealous of what we were doing, completely the opposite to what the interviewer had been told. It seemed that he had made up his mind about what he was going to write before the interview. This was a total fabrication and I was fuming. I went to see Jess and asked him to write to the paper and complain.

Jess didn't agree that we should. "This will do you nothing but good for the family. No, we won't complain. You just see what happens."

He proved to be right. First of all we got neighbours coming round to the house asking who had said these awful things. Then, at one of the concerts we were doing in Glasshoughton for the old age pensioners at the club, one of the committee members who I had known for years got up on stage and thanked us for the show and then started to lay into what he called trouble causers. He told everybody how he had seen our family grow up, how good they all were and finally threw out a challenge to whoever had spoken to the papers to come and say it to him personally. I hadn't the heart to tell him the reporter had written it that way to make a story.

Prior to the actual showing of the Christmas spectacular we were all invited down to London for the weekend and a promotional lunch at the Savoy Hotel. Photographs were taken on the Thames embankment for the TV Times Christmas edition and every entertainer who was popular at the time was invited. Sylvia, Glyn and myself had the pleasure of walking along the bank of the river chatting away to Petula Clark.

It was all very grand. Inside the hotel we tucked into steak and kidney pudding, washing it down with champagne and when I went to the toilet a gentleman in uniform filled up the sink for me and handed me a towel to dry my hands. Just like home really!

*

One day close to his retirement from work, Les Smalley phoned me and asked, "Would it be alright for me to come round and talk to you and Sylvia. I've received a letter which is anonymous and threatening and I would like you to see it. It's something that cannot be discussed over the telephone."

Les never had a lot of colour in his cheeks but when he walked into our house that night his face was ashen and deadly serious.

"Take a look at this. I think we should inform the police."

Both Sylvia and I read the letter. It was anonymous and the writing was almost illegible, almost like a child's writing. Clearly it was the product of some crank who was trying to scare us, but we all agreed it could not be ignored. The letter said that the writer would be at one of our next live events and would take care of Glyn and stop him singing for ever.

At the police station the desk sergeant read it and passed us on to a young man in plain clothes. Detective Constable Hirst looked at us and asked, "Which is Mr Smalley?"

Les nodded.

"So the letter was sent to you. Now then, first of all have you any idea of who might bear a grudge against you or Glyn?"

Les answered that he didn't think we or Glyn had an enemy in the world.

That's when we got our police escort. It was decided that detectives would accompany us at all our forthcoming events and anywhere Glyn would be exposed to the public. This went on for weeks. The very first outing following receipt of the letter was at a garden fete for Pinderfields Hospital at Stanley, near Wakefield. There were thousands there and sure enough the detectives kept very close to Glyn. Even when he opened the proceedings they were standing by his side looking closely at the crowd. Every time we turned out to go to a concert, an unmarked police car tagged on behind us. We had given them our dates and venues and they never missed. One show was at the Royal Hall, Harrogate. It was absolutely packed but two large, burly detectives were there trying to keep tabs on Glyn. As we stood on the balcony watching the old time music hall act which opened the show, Glyn watched, wrapping himself inside some very long velvet curtains. One of the detectives asked, "How the bloody hell do you watch him?"

*

During the summer of 1973 Stars on Sunday was to have a season at the Futurist Theatre in Scarborough. It had been sponsored by the Grades of London and would have Moira Anderson topping the bill. Jess was initially producing the television show but Equity, the Entertainers' Union, had agreed to let Jess present the show from the organ console. It

41

was a lovely show which lasted for thirteen weeks, and right through the summer season we played to packed houses.

As support Jess brought in The Wheatsheaf Girls' Choir, The York Celebration Choir, Bobby Bennet and Bev Jones. It was exactly what the holiday makers wanted to see.

During the Futurist summer season a traffic warden came into the dressing room. This surprised me as we couldn't see how we could be in trouble for parking as we were parked on the roof of the theatre. He put our minds at rest by asking if we could put our show on at the Floral Hall Theatre in Scarborough later in the year in aid of the Save the Children Fund. This was duly arranged for October after the summer shows had finished. Again I had the job of putting the show together and once again we incorporated Jean Pearce and her dancers. John Dawson did the lighting and gave advice to the theatre's sound man as to how and where we would like the mikes on stage. Once when we had a full bus of talented people waiting outside our house on the Sunday morning, we were just about to set off when the telephone rang. It was Mr Bland, my manager at Marks and Spencer's.

"I wonder if you could come down to the store with me to witness changing a dress for my wife? You see, we purchased it on Saturday night and it's the wrong size."

The reason for him asking me to help was because I was the only other store key holder and no-one was allowed to enter the store unaccompanied after closing, except in an emergency. I explained that I had a full concert party waiting outside but he sounded pretty desperate. I agreed to help him out. A bus full of dancers stood outside Marks and Spencers' in Carlton Street while Mrs Bland chose a new dress.

At the theatre we were greeted by the Mayor of Scarborough, Mr Jaconelli of ice cream and restaurant fame. That night we raised a lot of money, the show was a sell-out. After the show the coach driver was instructed to take the entire cast down to one of Mr Jaconelli's restaurants. We had a lovely meal which finished off with special ice cream.

*

Following the success of the live shows in Scarborough, Jess invited us to take part in one at the York Theatre Royal. The York Celebration Choir was in need of funds and Jess talked the Beverley Sisters into topping the bill.

I drove us all to the theatre and everybody went inside to the dressing rooms while I went off to park the minibus. When I came back and asked where they were, the man on the door told me to go up the stairs, turn left, turn right, and so on.

I followed his instructions. I could hear the voices of the children and carried on in the direction of the sounds. Up and up I went, then through a door. Suddenly I found myself going through a dark little room. It felt very creepy but I carried on, listening to the children's voices. Eventually I found I was right up in the gods, looking down on the stage from a great height. Back down the stairs I went. The dressing rooms were just below where I had been.

During the interval someone mentioned the Grey Lady. I asked, "What Grey Lady?" I asked.

"It's a story," he said, "that goes back to when some students were visiting the theatre. Two of them had been sitting up in the gods and one of them went to the toilet. The other, who was still watching the show, was suddenly aware of a grey, frail old lady sitting next to him. His friend came back and the figure faded away. Most sightings of the dear old lady are up in the gods."

He pointed to where I had been and talked about the room. I remembered the creepy feeling I had experienced.

The show went on to be a great success and the York Celebration Choir were able to continue for another year.

Letters were always arriving requesting our services for different occasions, mainly to help raise funds for the building of village halls. Unlike the towns and cities, local people got closely involved with projects for their community and everyone would pull together to achieve their aims. Once we received a letter from Wheldrake, a village near York. In the letter the organiser explained that they had been working hard to raise funds to enable them to build a new village hall and that they would like the Poole Family to open the new building in November that year when it was scheduled for completion.

When the time came for us to do the performance, we arrived at the new building and were greeted by the president of the project and his committee. He introduced us to the committee members and then said, "Thank you very much for coming, but before we go inside I have a confession to make. When they finished the building of the main hall last week they said they wouldn't be able to build the dressing rooms in time for this concert, so we have made you two dressing rooms at either side of the stage - from bales of straw. Have a look. I just hope you approve."

With that we went into the beautiful concert hall, all decorated in bright colours, the new stage complete with lighting. It was marvellous considering they'd had to start from scratch to raise the money.

"Now this is what we've done." At that he showed us the make-shift dressing rooms. Each was beautiful, the area about eight foot square, and enough headroom for us to climb up three steps to reach stage level. These rooms were thickly lined with compact bails of straw, each bail being about a yard square and over the top there was a double covering of tarpaulin. From the roof they had hung the lights.

"We've had the hot air blowers on all day to make sure of it being warm for you and the children," he said. The poor man was so relieved when we told him it was perfect. I think he'd been worrying about it all day. The kids thought it was marvellous and started off the evening by singing songs from Annie Get Your Gun. The show was good and everything was so different because of the make-shift dressing rooms. It all added to making it a very happy evening which was rounded off with a slap-up home baked buffet. By any standards it was a night to remember.

*

In those days our lives were pretty unpredictable; one day nothing and the next so packed we wondered if we could fit it all in. We did our share of working men's clubs and we were eternally grateful for the opportunities, but that was a more difficult world.

Anyone will tell you that clubland is the grass roots of entertainment but it's really more for the hardcore entertainers, not for a close family group who had never intended getting into serious entertainment in the first place. In the clubs we were sometimes playing second on the bill to bingo and it was only when the last game had been played that you discovered just how many had really come to hear you.

My brother Les was concert secretary at a club nearby and it was only natural that he wanted to engage his brother's family. We were very happy to oblige and we performed at his club three times and we were made very welcome. Success meant that on one occasion we were invited to be guest artists at the local concert secretaries' annual meeting. This meeting was where all concert secretaries met to talk about future entertainment, discuss artists and report any bad behaviour. We were spared the nitty-gritty of the formal meeting and afterwards we were asked to do our half hour spot. The chairman thanked us and as we came off the stage one concert secretary came up to Ted and then another and, to our amazement, a very long queue started to form. We had to explain about the limitations on the performance licences and I don't know how we sorted out who we could work for and who we couldn't, but in the end we satisfied everybody one way or another. Looking back at my own earlier career in clubland, I am sure that these concert secretaries would not have queued up the same for me.

Fame is a strange thing and the children got their taste of it early, but they were sensible enough to keep things in perspective. Once Michael was busy signing autographs after one village hall concert. A few young girls were around him and one girl in particular insisted that he signed her brand-new suede handbag. She asked him to put Duck Harry on the bag.

"Are you sure?" Michael asked.

"Yes," she insisted.

Michael duly signed the bag and the poor girl looked on in amazement as he wrote the words. Then her face changed.

"What are you doing?" she demanded.

"You said Duck Harry," Michael replied.

"No! I said to Karen."

Poor Mike couldn't wait to get out of the hall.

*

People in Castleford kept asking me when we were putting on another show. This gave me the idea for a charity show based on the Stars on Sunday format. I booked the Civic Centre but when I discussed it with Jess he said that for copyright reasons we would need to use some name other than Stars on Sunday. Sunday Stars and the Civic was chosen. Jess had used various small choirs to make one big choir, so I decided to form a united choir for the evening to give the show its Stars on Sunday identity.

Bas Phillips had all the contacts and without his help the show would never have got off the ground. Bev Jones, who had been working as musical director for Stars on Sunday had done musical arrangements for our children and agreed to help the York Singers. The Gott Sisters, the young concert pianists from Harrogate, also agreed to come. We also asked Carol Herbert, a young soprano from Leeds who took a lead part singing in the Holy City at the live show in Scarborough. To this array we added the trio: Bas, Jack Moulding and Ian Glenn, and John Dawson organised the lighting and sound.

After a lot of thought I decided to use one of Jess' ideas again and try to present the show from a different angle. This is where the Reverend

John McCarthy came in. I had a podium built for him just in front of the stage and spotlighted it during introductions.

The show was a sellout, opening with the United Featherstone Choir. Then the Gott Sisters gave a piano recital.

John McCarthy had done his homework on all the artists and said something about everyone. It was just right. Bev Jones did his version of Old Man River and his York singers gave a lovely performance of barber shop medleys and old folk songs. When the Poole Family came on the applause was terrific. We sang The Rhythm of Life from Sweet Charity. The money raised was donated to the charities nominated by Bas Phillips' Featherstone choirs.

*

In the course of my work at Marks and Spencer's, I was sometimes required to work nights. Because I was the local key holder for the store I was responsible for the security when contractors were working after the store had closed. Painters would arrive at about six o'clock in the evening, put sheets over all the counters, then work through until the early delivery warehouseman came on duty at six o'clock the next morning. That was when I could go home to bed.

On this particular Friday night there was a phone call for me at work. It was Sylvia. Her voice was faint and quavering.

"Cyril, I'm having to speak soft because Martin Phillips is in the other room."

"What's wrong?" I asked.

It was silent for a bit and then she said, "It's Bas. John McCarthy has just rung to tell us he's dead. He was on his way to choir practice. He was only yards away from Wilson Street Chapel when he collapsed. It was dark. John happened to come along the same way and almost stumbled over this figure on the ground."

Shocked, I said, "But I only spoke to him yesterday and he was fine then."

"He appears to have choked on a mint," said Sylvia.

I remembered that on our way to shows Bas would stop and buy extra strong mints. He used to hand them all round the bus. He said they were good for concentration.

"Oh, my God! Them bloody mints!" was all I could say before I broke down.

"Martin's staying the night," said Sylvia.

He and Stephen had planned to go to the football match the following day. "I haven't said anything to him yet. John will break the news to him in the morning."

The church and the crematorium were packed for the funeral. The Featherstone and District Amateur Musical and Dramatic Society, the Girnhill Singers, the Featherstone and District Male Voice Choir and all Bas' colleagues from Allerton Workshops were all there. As the funeral procession moved along, the streets of Featherstone were lined with people who had come to pay their respects to this fine and talented man.

*

How do you replace such a man? Well, maybe God was watching because out of the blue one Sunday morning an old mate, Harold Waite, from the buses called round. Harold had been my driver for seven years and I told him what had happened. He told me about a pianist who lived nearby and played at the local club. We quickly arranged to pay him a visit.

Terry Brearly was an architect by profession who lived on Pontefract Road in a big house with a grand piano in the lounge. When we asked him to help us out he agreed to give it a go.

Rehearsals started almost immediately. We had to learn to work with him but we found him to be very adaptable. Terry was a quietly spoken man with definite ideas on music; he was heaven-sent.

Our next big project was a concert at the Castleford Civic Centre to be called A Tribute to Basil Phillips. It allowed us to tap into all the choirs Bas had been involved with and the concert was to raise money to give to Margaret, his widow, as a mark of appreciation for Bas and his music. Carlton Main Frickley Band from Doncaster agreed to give their services just for the price of a coach and the Wheatsheaf Girls' Choir came along too.

The Civic Centre was packed. The Reverend John McCarthy worked from the podium and Ray Jarman and I wrote an obituary. Bas always loved The Chorus of the Slaves of Nabucco, a piece of opera that had been translated into a choir piece entitled Speed your Journey. The effect was very moving. The lights were dimmed, the recording boomed out over the audience and Ray delivered a tribute to this local musical hero.

The family together in Castleford

The Poole Family entourage

CHAPTER 5

We had been through all the various stages of development with our family, each child learning to walk, talk and then starting school. But now they were growing up and Stephen and Wendy were ready to start work. We felt that they needed somewhere to entertain their own friends, so in 1972 we decided to move into Ferrybridge Road.

We had always been a close family so Stephen moving on was a big step. The Leeds and Holbeck Building Society gave him his first job. To us he didn't look big enough to be starting work but, before we knew it there he was, four foot nothing and travelling with the city gents into the great big world of work.

"Now then, how have you gone on?" Sylvia asked when he returned from his first day.

"Alright. But I was sick on the train. Everybody was nice to me though."

"Well, what's it like to be a working man?" I asked, not really knowing what to say.

"I've enjoyed it," he said.

Then it was Wendy's turn. We took her to Wakefield for her interview at E Green and Sons, Economizes, an engineering company who made machinery for the coal mines in the area. She got it. Two down, five to go.

As Stephen and Wendy grew up they became more self-conscious and their enthusiasm for going out singing with the family waned. Jess noticed this and drew our attention to it.

'I don't think we will use the oldest two on the show any more. Anyway, it's going to be difficult for them to get time off work.'

When we told Stephen and Wendy, we sensed their relief.

*

The Easter holiday 1974 had started normally enough. I'd been doing a bit of decorating when out of the blue came a telephone call. Deke Arlon, our recording manager at York Records, wanted to know if Glyn would be interested in making a single. He felt the time was right for Glyn after Jimmy Osmond's success with Long Haired Lover from Liverpool and

Michael Jackson's Ben.

I agreed straight away and when I told Sylvia and the rest of the family they were all very excited. A short-list of four songs was sent through the post - Naomi, Beautiful City, Sunday Afternoon Boat Ride and Milly, Molly, Mandy. When Ivor Raymonde, the record producer, arrived at our house from London a week later, Glyn was word perfect. Ivor, a typical cockney with no airs and graces and really down to earth, was an established professional. He had already produced Neil Reid's number one Mother of Mine and a string of sixties hits, so we felt Glyn was in good hands. A couple of weeks later, Glyn and Sylvia travelled down to London for the recordings. The recording was done at the Nova studios and afterwards Ivor was so pleased with Glyn he took him and Sylvia out to dinner right at the very top of the famous Post Office Tower.

They arrived home full of stories about the recording and how well they had been treated. Dick Rowe, who had done the mixing for the records, had given Sylvia a demo tape of the four songs and when we played them to some close friends they were all so good none of us could agree which we thought should be chosen. Eventually news came through that Milly, Molly, Mandy was the choice, with Beautiful City for the 'B' side. A release date for October 1974 had been decided and they sent us some BBC play lists. These are the lists which are approved by the producers of chart programmes. The record company representatives have to put in a lot of work to persuade these producers that the material on the records is what their listeners want. If there is agreement then the producers send the record company the dates and times they intend playing the record.

Hearing the record for the first time on Ed Stewart's Junior Choice programme was very exciting. Then 'Diddy' David Hamilton started to plug it on his afternoon show, singing along and encouraging listeners to do the same. Junior Choice was broadcast early on Saturday and Sunday mornings and Sylvia used to dance round the bedroom to the record. Before long it was 'bubbling under the charts', as they say in the record business. It means that through record sales and surveys by chart list analysts, the record is rated in the top forty.

By then people in high places had begun to sit up and take notice. Sylvia and Glyn were invited down to London for publicity meetings. Following these, Glyn was interviewed on Radio One, Capital Radio, by the national press and various magazine reporters. It looked as though York Records had a hit on their hands.

By November the record was number 31 in the charts and excitement was really growing. The record company decided to make an LP on the strength of what was happening. Another eight songs were chosen and Glyn, Sylvia and myself went down to London again, first to accompany Glyn when making the tracks and then to meet Deke Arlon, the recording manager. I was surprised to see how young he was and when he introduced us to a representative of a London agency who looked after recording artists all over the world and began explaining the intricacies of contracts, I began to feel a sense of unease. These people were asking Sylvia and I to put our children's lives completely in their hands. I just couldn't think straight. How do you sign away the right to look after your children's affairs just like that? Who were these people and who gave them the right to interfere with our family? The fact of the matter was that I was afraid of losing control and so we were very cautious and refused to be rushed in to signing anything.

We seemed to talk for ages. Deke Arlon encouraged me to take this very professional step, but both Sylvia and I were thinking more positively and from a parent's point of view. In the end our love and family bond made us take a negative approach to recording. Even though we enjoyed the limelight, we were not ready to sign any of our family's rights away and then live to regret it. We were concerned that once in the hands of these people, it could be difficult to get out if things went wrong.

Both Sylvia and I travelled home on the train with our heads buzzing, wondering if we had said the right things. This world of the big stars was more complicated than ordinary mortals could take in.

The following weekend we were in a Castleford record shop and Glyn was signing autographs. That's when it was really exciting. It was wonderful to see so many local people turning out in our home town and queuing up to buy the record. From there it was next stop Leeds and another wonderful reception. This promotion shot the record to number one in the West Riding charts although it was still holding at 31 in the national charts.

The same weekend Barry Johnson, the publicity bloke from York Records, took us across to Liverpool for an interview on Radio Merseyside. The presenter of the programme was a real Scouse who told us all about the days when the Beatles had played at the Cavern and how he had been involved in the early days before their rise to fame.

Then he introduced Glyn: "Well, good evening to you out there. If you're looking for England's answer to Jimmy Osmond, here he is. An up and coming local lad. Only twelve years old but he has taken the charts by storm with Milly, Molly, Mandy and is about to release his first LP."

With this he moved the sound slide on his control panel to bring in one of Glyn's tracks from the LP, then he turned to us and said, "Right Glyn. When the record's finished I'll ask you a few questions about yourself and about making the records and we'll take it from there."

The interview went well and before we left Liverpool he took us to his night club right in the heart of Liverpool. It was early evening, there was no-one there so he was able to show us his stage that came up at the press of a button out of the middle of the dance floor. It gave us an interesting insight into Liverpool's night life.

Next day it was across the M62 to Radio Humberside where another interview took place for an East Yorkshire audience. We also visited radio stations in Sheffield and Leeds and the record distribution depot in Manchester where we met all the staff who would be handling Glyn's record. Barry had thought of everything.

The next publicity plan he had arranged was something completely different. The following week he rang to ask if we would be at home on Friday evening. We told him we would be, but he didn't enlighten us as to what was to happen. He told us some press people would be coming to take some interesting photos of Glyn. Friday evening came round and none of the children wanted to miss anything so nobody went out, not even the older children. At about seven-thirty two large cars pulled up outside and out came three men, one who was obviously a photographer. Then they opened the back of one of the cars and lifted out three monkeys, a mother and two babies. They each had T-shirts on. The older one had Milly printed right across her chest, and the others Molly and Mandy. They had come from Flamingo Park - Yorkshire Television had shares in the leisure park - and they were using the monkeys for publicity.

The photographer sat Glyn at the piano with a copy of the music but when they tried to sit the monkeys on the top of the piano the older one started hitting Glyn on the top of the head. The younger ones were less active, they just took bites out of the piano top. As the keepers fought for control the older one reached down, picked up the music and threw it across the room. We all watched in amazement. After a while one of the keepers said, "I think I know what's up. She wants a smoke."

To our shock and further amazement he picked her up and took her outside. He swung her on Sylvia's washing line, lit up and gave the monkey the cigarette. We all stood with our mouths wide open as she puffed away with one hand and swung up and down on the line with the other. When eventually they came inside it had quietened her and they managed to get some pictures.

By December, the single was still at number 31. To push things along York Records decided to go for a wider audience and the week before Christmas Glyn and Sylvia were flown out to Germany to record Milly, Molly, Mandy in German. It was called Liebe Rosalinda and was mugged up by Glyn from a translation tape. The trip to the Munich studios was a nice mini-holiday for them both. Glyn, who by now was known as 'one-take Glyn', did a good job with the recording.

Still the pressure for sales went on. Back in London, Barry Johnson had arranged for Ed Stewart to take us to lunch before visiting Westminster Children's Hospital. Ed was dressed in his Buttons pantomime gear and with Glyn he went round the children's ward giving out presents and LPs, signing plaster casts and having fun with the kids.

After that and having said goodbye to Ed Stewart, we went to Chelsea where 'Diddy' David Hamilton was playing in a charity football game. We watched the first half of the game and were able to have a word with him at half time. Our intention was to ask for air play on his programme for the tracks from the LP. He was very enthusiastic about Milly, Molly, Mandy and said that if the tracks on the LP were half as good they wouldn't need much plugging. He was very friendly and had photographs taken with Glyn.

Then it was my turn to go with Glyn to Germany for publicity. David Jefferson, the manager of York Records, accompanied us armed with LPs for distribution in the British Forces area.

The publicity man from the German record company was John Newton who originated from Huddersfield but had spent most of his working life in Hamburg as a recording publicity manager. He was a very nice chap and, after the initial greetings, soon involved us with the job in hand as we had a very tight schedule. Our first visit was to the very famous broadcasting studios in the heart of Luxemburg. Glyn was introduced to a German presenter who interviewed him over the radio and translated his answers to the German audience. He referred to us as, "Herr Varter Poole und kleiner Glyn Poole." For lunch we had Wiener Schnitzel and drank German red wine.

After lunch we went to the other side of the studio for Radio Luxemburg. There the presenter was Tony Prince, a very English lad who was well up with the English charts and knew all about Glyn. We all sat at an old round broadcasting table which looked a bit worse for wear.

It had a faded baize covering and various holes in for mike connections. I was amazed by the squalor but Tony explained to us, "The reason that this studio is preserved in this state is because it was from here that William Joyce as Lord Haw Haw made his many war time propaganda broadcasts to the British people. They later hanged him."

The photo session took place on the banks of the Rhine in very picturesque and beautiful settings. We spent a whole day by the Rhine and had lunch in a posh hotel.

The next stop was BFPO Cologne where all the English troops and their families were based. We visited a school and sang with the children, then visited another radio station which was the British Forces Network for the BBC. Glyn was interviewed and his English version of Milly, Molly, Mandy was played followed by the German version Liebe Rosalinda. After leaving the studio John Newton informed us that we had the rest of the day to ourselves, but we wouldn't have known where to go or what to see. However John had generously organised a tour of Cologne Cathedral and took us down into the vaults to see the Cathedral's gold treasures. He then took us up the spiral staircase to the top of one of its towers for a wonderful view of Cologne. It was a fantastic experience but it didn't make Glyn an international celebrity.

Gradually Glyn's record slipped out of the charts, the LP didn't do a great deal and we didn't hear any more from Germany so we presumed that we hadn't reached the charts over there. But what an experience for an ordinary Glasshoughton lad.

*

On our return Jess rang me up. "I'm thinking of doing a double take using some of your kids' earlier recordings so if they can come into the studio we can have them singing along with it. I've had a lot of mail asking about the Poole Family and I want to show them how they have all grown up."

So it was arranged. Stephen and Wendy got involved too and we all did a recording of Shall we Gather at the River. Jess introduced the children with a bit of history about the family starting with the original recording and then showing the family as we were five years on. It worked a treat and letters were received in response to it.

It seemed at the time to be just what the family needed if we were to continue in show business. However just as things were on the move, Jess Yates was hitting the front pages of every newspaper but for all the wrong reasons. He was having an affair with a young dancer. The press had a field day because of Stars on Sunday. They ran headlines like The Bishop and the Showgirl and crucified him. The pressure was so great that on one occasion it led to him leaving the studios in the boot of a car to avoid the waiting journalists who followed his every move.

Sylvia and I had met the young girl in question, we'd had tea at the studios with her and her parents. Jess' marriage appeared to be in name only, he had one daughter who suffered from asthma and lived with her mother in Malta. He had only spoken about his wife a few times and, because of his work and the distance between them, we knew that something wasn't quite right. His relationship with Anita Kay was really like father and daughter, although she did try to mother him. However, the unusual nature of the relationship didn't fit in with his Stars on Sunday image. He was hounded by the press and eventually someone decided that he had to go.

This was a sad blow for anyone who had anything to do with Jess. Yorkshire Television were committed to finishing both of Jess' programmes and Peter Max Wilson, who had been Jess' understudy for years, was given the job of completing them. Our family was involved in both Junior Showtime and Stars on Sunday but we got the feeling we would not be asked back again. Our guess proved to be right.

When you are not on television, people quickly forget about you. Gradually we stopped getting requests for shows but we didn't have much time to think about it. With a family of our size there can be no dull moments, it just meant more time to be an ordinary family again. Friends used to refer to us affectionately as rent-a-crowd and that's what we became, though this time for a smaller circle of people.

Denise, Judith and Angela were members of the local youth club. They used to bring home lots of friends and among them would be the occasional boyfriend. Michael, who was now at art college, always brought home two or three friends from the youth club and they would spend all evening playing heavy metal on their guitars in the front room. Wendy, being the oldest girl, had a steady boyfriend, Paul who was a rugby footballer. Stephen began to go out to night clubs with Ian Glen and he even began to take a pride in his appearance which hadn't bothered him before, and he started using my Brut aftershave which I put down to growing up. So the numbers doubled and sometimes trebled; it seemed as though our house was a good meeting place for them all.

It was not unusual for us all to pack into our mini bus, Sylvia would fix up a picnic for us and off we would go to places like Brimham Rocks where we would play simple games like hide and seek among the rocks, a game that would last all day, only breaking for the sandwiches. Most of our children's friends had no brothers or sisters, unlike our lot, and they seemed to love the large family atmosphere.

Because of their connections with the Castleford Centre XI Youth Club, some of our children took part in reviews and the rock musical Joseph and his Amazing Technicolour Dreamcoat. The youth club was fortunate to have Bob Hewitt as its senior youth officer. He was also a musician and was able to produce these shows. He encouraged other kids who could play instruments to help with the accompaniment.

It was through Bob and his wife, Trish, that we were to take our first holiday on the island of Anglesey just off North Wales. Bob was originally to take a youth party on a camping holiday when he found he was suddenly short of adult helpers. He asked our children, some of whom were going anyway, "Do you think your Mam and Dad would be interested in coming with us?"

After a few discussions with him we decided to take up the offer. We hadn't booked anywhere ourselves and, as the youth club had plenty of tents available, we could take the whole family.

It was a very hot fortnight and we had lots of fun. Bob had taken a dinghy with an outboard motor along which added to the enjoyment. One of the highlights of the holiday was a trip across to a small island which we christened 'Sagu Island' after we had said many times, "Who wants sagu across to the island?" The Boys' Brigade were camping in the next field. Each morning we were woken up by the sound of their bugle, but we got our own back. I found an old bugle and had great fun standing on the top of the mini bus, blowing it loudly.

This was to prove to be a very memorable holiday for us all. We sometimes meet some of those kids from the youth club who are now grown up, but they always refer to the holiday as great.

As I have mentioned earlier, Stephen our eldest son had suddenly grown up, we had noticed him washing his hair regularly. This was the lad whose only interest had been sport and now he had met a girl and he calmly announced that he wanted to get married.

So here we were starting another phase in our lives, preparing for our son's wedding and hoping that he had made the right choice of partner.

The wedding was planned for July 1975 and was just like any other wedding - no big stars or anybody important other than the families involved. Tony Hill came up from Bath, he had always kept in touch with Stephen and he took some of our kids in his Rolls Royce to pick strawberries for the reception. Sylvia and some friends were doing the reception which was held in the chapel school rooms.

Most appropriately the Reverend John McCarthy performed the ceremony. Stephen and his new wife Julie purchased a little house in Castleford and so the first of the Poole family had finally flown the nest.

We did hear from Jess in the autumn of 1975 and he asked us if we would help him out with some live shows he was going to do the following year. We explained to him we hadn't been doing any live shows and we no longer had a pianist. Terry Brearly, being a semi-professional organist, had now got other regular engagements. However when we asked Bob Hewitt, the youth leader, he agreed to play for us. The first show was at Easter in Blackpool on the Central Pier. It was called A Night with Jess Yates and Friends. Jean Pearce brought her dancers and The Beverley Sisters topped the bill. Jess told us that if this was a success then he had a chance to do a full summer season of Sunday shows at the Llandudno Astra Theatre. We all agreed to take part, after all it kept the family name going and it would be enjoyable doing a summer season again.

We did thirteen weeks at the Astra in the hot summer of 1976 and it was a great success. Jess had a different star topping the bill every week. We enjoyed it very much and combined it with another two weeks' camping holiday on Anglesey because we had enjoyed the previous holiday so much. During that holiday Jess invited us up to his house just outside Conway for a weekend and Anita, who was still with him, fed us and made us very welcome.

During our stay at Jess', Wendy phoned us to say that John Dawson had come off his motorbike while answering a police emergency call. We learned later that he died in hospital from his injuries. John had a massive funeral with full police honours and the chief of West Yorkshire Police in attendance. John's death was a great loss to his widow and two small children and also to many people in the world of entertainment.

*

1976 was a very significant year in our lives. I had been having trouble with my ears and suffered from vertigo. I'd had quite a lot of attacks causing me to fall down suddenly and I even fell down while sitting, which is very hard to explain. When I eventually saw an ear specialist, Mr Peter Mills, at St James' Hospital in Leeds, he explained to me I had been going deaf in my left ear for a long time, in fact my hearing was almost non-existent. After several long and uncomfortable tests, he diagnosed Menieurs Disease. Mr Mills decided that the only way was to operate and destroy the left labyrinth which would terminate my hearing in my left ear altogether. He arranged for me to go into hospital and, using micro surgery, he performed the very delicate operation a week later.

The operation was a success and after ten weeks' therapy, virtually learning to regain my balance and walk a straight line, I recovered but had to contend with the fact that I now only had hearing in my right ear. Because of this, the pressure at Marks and Spencer's was a bit too much for me. Mr Mills had pointed out that I should avoid stress if possible, so Sylvia and I decided to look for some sort of job where we could work together and she could help me with any hearing difficulties.

Our first choice was to take a pub, maybe one where we could do some entertainment along with managing the bar. But that didn't come to fruition straight away, so we decided to take a fish shop. But before we left Ferrybridge Road in October of 1976, Wendy and her boyfriend had decided they were getting married. Paul, her boyfriend of the last few years, had travelled with us to many concerts when Wendy was still singing with the family. They were already engaged and he was very much part of the Poole family, so it came as no surprise when they announced their intentions.

Once again the family machine went into action preparing for a September wedding. Because Paul also came from a large family, this wedding was a little bit bigger than Stephen's and, of course, Paul's football friends were invited. I felt so proud with the first of my daughters looking so beautiful walking down the aisle of St Paul's Parish Church, and her day was a glorious one.

So now the Poole family nest was beginning to empty, our two eldest children had embarked on the long voyage of married life and now we were to plunge into the unknown world of fish shops.

In the last few moments I spent in 96 Ferrybridge Road, I said goodbye to a lot of memories both happy and sad. I often wonder if that house still thrives on the sound of music.

Cyril Poole first approached Yorkshire Art Circus to produce his autobiography by learning word processing and desk top publishing skills in the weekly Art Circus Education sessions. His story was then produced as the first autobiography to come out of the Smawthorne and Glasshoughton community arts project and it celebrates the far from ordinary life of one Smawthorne family.

This book is published as part of a programme of community development associated with the Smawthorne and Glasshoughton Housing Renewal Scheme. In a unique collaboration over the last two years, Yorkshire Art Circus has been working for Wakefield MDC Housing Services to demonstrate that arts skills can help forge a link between local authority and community. The result has been an innovative programme of publications and events.

Yorkshire Art Circus works to increase access to writing and publishing and to develop new models of practice for arts in the community. Yorkshire Art Circus is a registered charity.

Art Circus Education (ACE) is arts based practical training in an informal workplace atmosphere. It combines traditional skills like story-telling, writing and craft techniques with new technology and works towards an end product.